To

From

DEDICATED TO THE LIFE OF

JOHN WILLIAM HICKS,

THE DASH BETWEEN

JUNE 12, 1930 - JULY 5, 2004.

DAD, I'LL LOVE YOU FOREVER.

LINDA

The Dash

Making a Difference with Your Life

~❧~

by Linda Ellis and Mac Anderson

Published by Simple Truths, LLC
1952 McDowell Road, Suite 300
Naperville, IL 60563
800-900-3427

Photo Credits:

Steve Terrill *(www.terrillphoto.com)* Front cover, and pages 9, 11, 12, 14, 16,
18, 20, 22, 24, 26, 28, 30, 32, 34, 36, 38, 42, 45, 48, 52, 55, 59, 66, 68, 72, 75,
78, 82, 83, 85, 86.

Bruce Heinemann *(www.theartofnature.com)* pages 71, 91.

Todd Reed *(www.toddreedphoto.com)* pages 80, 84.

ISBN 978-1-60810-032-3

Design: Rich Nickel
Editor: Jennifer Svoboda

Printed and bound in the United States of America

www.simpletruths.com

08 WOZ 11

Table of Contents

Introduction

The letter hit my desk on June 10, 2003. I opened it to see a short, handwritten note attached to a single sheet of paper. The note was from Anna Lee Wilson, a Successories franchisee from Evansville, Indiana. She thanked me for speaking the week before at the grand opening of her new restaurant, and at the bottom of the note was a post script that read: "I know you have inspirational poems, and this is my all-time favorite. It's titled, *The Dash,* by Linda Ellis." Well, first of all, when Anna Lee speaks, I listen, because she is one of the kindest, most caring people I've ever met. I knew if it was her favorite, it had to be good.

I can count on one hand how many times I've read something that stopped me in my tracks...words that bypassed the brain and went straight to the heart. This was one of those moments. It was one of those times when I immediately thought...how could I use my talents to share these powerful, thought-provoking words with the rest of the world?

The first step was to contact the author, Linda Ellis. She answered the phone, and I introduced myself, and told her how much I love her poem. She then told me her story about how, in one afternoon in 1996, she was inspired to write *The Dash*. Her life, she said, has not been the same since then.

Introduction

Life works in strange ways. But I feel this project was meant to be. Joseph Epstein once said, "We do not choose to be born. We do not choose our parents, or the country of our birth. We do not, most of us, choose to die; nor do we choose the time and conditions of our death. But within this realm of choicelessness, we do choose how we live."

This is what *The Dash* is all about.

Read it! Enjoy it! And, just one more thing…make someone's day by sharing it.

Live with passion,

Mac Anderson
Founder, Successories and Simple Truths

The Dash

By Linda Ellis

I read of a man who stood to speak

at the funeral of a friend.

He referred to the dates on her tombstone

from the beginning...to the end.

He noted that first came the date of her birth

and spoke of the following date with tears,

but he said what mattered most of all…

was the dash between those years.

For that dash represents all the time

that she spent alive on earth

and now only those who loved her

know what that little line is worth.

For it matters not, how much we own,

the cars...the house...the cash...

What matters is how we live and love...

and how we spend our dash.

So think about this long and hard;

are there things you'd like to change?

For you never know how much time is left

that can still be rearranged.

If we could just slow down enough

to consider what's true and real...

and always try to understand

the way other people feel.

And be less quick to anger

and show appreciation more

and love the people in our lives...

like we've never loved before.

If we treat each other with respect

and more often wear a smile…

remembering that this special dash

might only last a little while.

So when your eulogy is being read...

with your life's actions to rehash…

would you be proud of the things they say...

about how you spent your dash?

The Dash

By Linda Ellis

I read of a man who stood to speak
at the funeral of a friend.
He referred to the dates on her tombstone
from the beginning…to the end.

He noted that first came the date of her birth
and spoke of the following date with tears,
but he said what mattered most of all
was the dash between those years.

For that dash represents all the time
that she spent alive on earth
and now only those who loved her
know what that little line is worth.

For it matters not, how much we own,
the cars…the house…the cash.
What matters is how we live and love
and how we spend our dash.

So think about this long and hard;
are there things you'd like to change?
For you never know how much time is left
that can still be rearranged.

If we could just slow down enough
to consider what's true and real
and always try to understand
the way other people feel.

And be less quick to anger
and show appreciation more
and love the people in our lives
like we've never loved before.

If we treat each other with respect
and more often wear a smile…
remembering that this special dash
might only last a little while.

So when your eulogy is being read
with your life's actions to rehash,
would you be proud of the things they say
about how you spent your dash?

How will you spend your Dash?

One of the most difficult lessons in life to learn is that…less, is usually more. And only as I've grown older, have I "gotten it." Focusing on your most important priorities, and continually removing the clutter, will be key to any true success in your life. That's what I love about this poem. In 239 words, it captures the "simple truths" of why we were put on this earth.

Sometimes, when you look through the lens of a camera, the image is blurred. However, with one small tweak of the lens, it can become crystal clear. For me, that's what can happen when combining a beautiful photograph with inspirational words…it can resonate with your imagination and bring the idea to life.

Within the words of this beautiful poem, I discovered a few simple truths that can make a difference in any life. I'd like to share them with you to help bring your "dash goals" into focus.

May you live your Dash with passion,

Mac Anderson

"If we could just *slow down*

enough to consider what's true and real..."

Slow Down

Ionce heard someone say, "We don't remember days; we remember moments." However, at today's hectic pace we often forget to savor small pleasures while we make big plans.

In the race to be better or best, we sometimes lose sight of "just being." And just being, just soaking in and savoring a beautiful moment, can provide some of life's greatest pleasures. A crackling fire on a cold winter night; a good book; a love letter from your spouse; a spectacular sunset; a great meal; or a timeless moment with your child or a friend…these moments, if we stop long enough to enjoy, are the essence of life.

Slow Down

I love to fish, especially for large-mouth bass. About three years ago, I was watching television late one night and got this crazy notion to go fishing in the lake behind my house. Of course, my wife thought I was nuts. It was almost midnight! I convinced her I was sane and took off. I walked out to a warm summer breeze and looked up at the starry sky and breathtaking full moon. I allowed my senses to soak in every second — the sweet smell of honeysuckle, the sound of every cricket and bullfrog, the moon's reflection dancing off the water — it was a perfect night.

After walking across a small field, I took out a flashlight and selected a lure. On my first cast, I reeled in a bass weighing over five pounds, one of the largest I had ever caught. I gently released it back into the water and continued my midnight adventure. During the next two hours, I caught seventeen bass, all between two and five pounds. Although I've fished for almost fifty years, no fishing memory can top that warm summer night.

But that night provided far more than a fishing memory. It was a life memory. It provided me a snapshot of what life could be like if I just slowed down enough to savor the moments. On my way back to the house, as I walked through the tall grass, I took one last look at the sky and stopped to say, "Thank you, God, for giving me this night."

Remember, it will only last for a little while…so savor the moments, savor the memories of your Dash.

"Every hour of every day is an unspeakably perfect miracle."
—WALT WHITMAN

True and

"If we could just slow down enough
to consider what's *true and real*..."

~❦~

True and Real

Knowing yourself, finding your true purpose in life, is the essence of true and real. "You have to be, before you do, to have lasting inner peace." In other words, making a living is not the same as making a life. Find what makes your heart sing and create your own music.

Many people work all their lives and dislike what they do for a living. In fact, I was astounded to see a recent *USA Today* survey that said 53 percent of people in the American workplace are unhappy with their jobs. Loving what you do is one of the most important keys to living a "true and real" Dash.

You can't fake passion. It is the fuel that drives any dream and makes you happy to be alive. However, the first step to loving what you do is to self analyze, to simply know what you love. We all have unique talents and interests, and one of life's greatest challenges is to match these talents with career opportunities that bring out the best in us. It's not easy — and sometimes we can only find it through trial and error — but it's worth the effort.

Ray Kroc, for example, found his passion when he founded McDonald's at the age of 52. He never "worked" another day of his life.

John James Audubon was unsuccessful for most of his life. He was a terrible businessman. No matter how many times he changed locations, changed partners, or changed businesses, he still failed miserably. Not until he understood that he must change himself did he have any shot at success.

And what changes did Audubon make? He followed his passion. He had always loved the outdoors and was an excellent hunter. In addition, he was a good artist and, as a hobby, would draw local birds.

Once he stopped trying to be a businessman and started doing what he loved to do, his life turned around. He traveled the country observing and drawing birds, and his art ultimately was collected in a book titled *Audubon's Birds of America*. The book earned him a place in history as the greatest wildlife artist ever. But more importantly, the work made him happy and provided the peace of mind he'd been seeking all his life.

*"Throw your heart over the fence
and the rest will follow."*

— NORMAN VINCENT PEALE

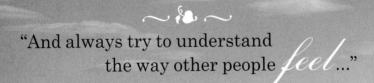

"And always try to understand
the way other people *feel*..."

Feelings

I once heard someone say, "If you teach your child the Golden Rule, you will have left them an incalculable estate." Truer words were never spoken.

More than anything, the Golden Rule is about kindness. As Mother Teresa said, "It's the only language that we all understand." John Blumberg, author, speaker and friend, recently told me a story that I'd like to share with you:

Feelings

"I had just experienced a pleasant flight from New York back to Chicago on United Airlines. It was one of those days where almost everything had gone right. That's until I exited the tram to the airport's economy parking lot and realized that I had lost my wallet on my homeward journey.

Throughout the drive home I mentally started retracing my steps. Once home, I placed calls to the "lost-and-found" at O'Hare, United, NY-LaGuardia and the TSA security in New York. At that late night hour I got recordings, so I left each a detailed message. I then retired to bed knowing I had done all I could do. I fell asleep thinking of the hassle of replacing everything in the wallet.

The next morning, I had been up for less than an hour when a man called. Bob identified himself with United Airlines, and his question was music to my ears — "Mr. Blumberg, are you missing a wallet?" Relieved and grateful, I responded, YES! I thanked him for returning my call to United's lost-and-found. But he didn't know about that call. He wasn't with the lost-and-found — nor was it his job to personally follow-up with passengers leaving their stuff on the airplane. He was the night mechanic who had simply found the wallet on my assigned seat. Realizing my phone number was not anywhere in my wallet, I immediately appreciated his extra effort of tracking down my home phone number. But that effort was only the beginning of what I was about to experience.

Bob had waited the night to call, assuming I would be sleeping. He told me that he was leaving work at 7:00 a.m. He wanted to know if I would be home so he could deliver my wallet to my house on his way home. After talking logistics for a minute, I realized that he was going over an hour out of his way. But he insisted. I finally got him to agree that I would immediately leave and meet him in a direction near his home. For the next 45-minutes, we both drove towards a common meeting place.

Feelings

We finally met in the parking lot of a commercial building. As I got out of my car to meet this stranger-turned-hero, I introduced myself to Bob. He sported his heavy United Airlines uniform coat made necessary by the cold December morning. He greeted me with a big smile and handed me my wallet. I pulled some cash from my pocket to give him a sizeable tip for all his efforts. As I reached to hand him the cash, he didn't miss a beat. He simply responded, "Absolutely not!"

Bob continued, "I have lost my wallet before and I know it is a hassle. I am just glad that I could get it back to you." Feeling the need to somehow respond to his kindness, I offered the tip a couple more times. But he was not budging. Realizing the tip minimized his graciousness, I just smiled and said, "I guess I will just have to pay-it-forward to someone else." He smiled, "That would be great." You see, Bob went the extra mile…and then some. He didn't do it for gain, he did it simply because it's who he is."

During our Dash on this earth, we all have countless opportunities to perform unexpected acts of kindness. Emerson said it best; "To share often and much…to know even one life has breathed easier because you have lived; this is to have succeeded."

"The true meaning of life is to plant trees under whose shade you do not expect to sit."
— NELSON HENDERSON

feelings

Anger

"And be less quick to *anger*
and show appreciation more."

Anger

Our emotions are powerful motivators, and more than almost anything else in our lives they will drive our behavior. Sometimes our greatest challenge is to get inside our own heads to understand what make us tick. Why do we feel and behave the way we do?

I know two family members who were best of friends, but several years ago, one reminded the other of something that had happened thirty years earlier. One thing led to another and, you know what, they haven't spoken since.

William Ward identified the cure when he said, "Forgiveness is the key that unlocks the handcuffs of hate."

Those are powerful words, and I know from personal experience...forgiveness works. A few times in my life I've been greatly wronged and taken advantage of. My first reaction, of course, was anger and resentment. I held it for awhile and felt my stomach tie up in knots, my appetite wane, and the joy slip out of my life.

The quote from Ward provided the wake-up call I needed to forgive the person who had wronged me. It was like I had been playing the first half of a basketball game with three-pound steel shoes, and in the locker room the coach said, "Mac, try these new Nikes in the  second half." Multiply that by ten and you'll understand how great it feels to unload your "emotional baggage" through the power of forgiveness.

Life is too short to stay angry…even for a day. Just remember that, "this special Dash may only last a little while."

> *"Forgiveness does not change the past,*
> *but it does enlarge the future."*

— PAUL BOESE

Appreciation

Barbara Glanz (www.barbaraglanz.com) is a speaker, author and also a good friend. One of her favorite quotes from Albert Schweitzer is: "Sometimes our light goes out but is blown again into flame by an encounter with another human being. Each of us owes the deepest thanks to those who have rekindled this inner light."

When Barbara speaks, she will ask her audience to shut their eyes and to think about someone who at some time in their lives has rekindled their inner light. She will leave the room in silence for several minutes, and it is always a profound experience for everyone as they remember the JOY they received from the appreciation of someone when they needed it the most.

"And be less quick to anger
and show *appreciation* more."

Afterwards, she'll ask them to write down the name of the person they thought of and to commit to their own act of appreciation by letting that person know in the next 72 hours that they thought of them. She'll suggest a phone call, a note, or even just a little prayer if they are no longer alive.

After one very moving session, a gentleman came up to talk with her and thank her for creating a new awareness in him. He said he had thought of his eighth grade literature teacher because she was everyone's favorite teacher and had really made a difference in all of their lives, and he was going to track her down and let her know what happened.

One afternoon nearly two and a half months later, Barbara received a call from him. He was very emotional on the phone and could hardly get through his story. He said that it had taken him nearly two months to track his teacher down, and when he finally found her, he wrote to her and the following week this was the letter he received back:

Dear John,

You will never know how much your letter meant to me. I am 83 years old, and I am living all alone in one room. My friends are all gone. My family's gone.

I taught for 50 years and yours is the first "thank you" letter I have ever gotten from a student. Sometimes I wonder what I did with my life. I will read and reread your letter until the day I die.

He sobbed on the phone. He said, "Every reunion we've had, she is always the one we talked about. She was everyone's favorite teacher – we loved her!"

But no one had ever told her…until she received his letter.*

Never forget…it is not the things you get, but the hearts you touch that will determine your success in your Dash.

~ ❦ ~

"What you leave behind is not what is engraved in stone monuments, but what is woven into the lives of others."

— PERICLES

"And love the people in our lives

like we've never *loved* before."

Love

I recently had dinner with someone who told me that one of his best friends had been killed in a private plane crash, and something happened at the service that he'll never forget. He shared the story with me.

At the memorial service, his friend's wife walked to the podium to speak to the gathering. She said a friend had asked her the best memory she had of their life together. At the moment, she had been too grief-stricken to answer, but she had thought about it since and wanted to answer the question.

They were in their late forties when he died, and she began talking about a time in their life almost twenty years earlier. She had quit her job to obtain her master's degree, and her husband never wavered in his support.

Love

He held down his own job and also did the cooking, cleaning, and other household chores while she studied for her degree.

One time they both stayed up all night. She was finishing her thesis, and he was preparing for an important business meeting. That morning, she walked out on their loft, looked at him over the railing, and just thought about how much she loved him. She knew how important this meeting was to his career, and she was feeling guilty that she didn't even have time to make his breakfast. He grabbed his briefcase and hurried out. She heard the garage door open and close, but much to her surprise, she heard it open again about thirty seconds later. From above, she watched her husband dash into the house and walk over to the neglected coffee table. Tracing his finger through the dust, he wrote the words, "I love you." Then he raced back to his car.

The new widow then looked out at her audience and said, "John and I had a wonderful life together. We have been around the world several times, we've had everything money can buy…but nothing comes close to that moment."

Our Dash moves with lightning speed. It feels like yesterday that I graduated from college…and now thirty-eight years have passed. Although I'm very proud of my business accomplishments, in the end my life comes back to loving and being loved.

"Love may not make the world go around
but it sure makes the ride worthwhile."

"Treat each other with *respect*
and more often wear a smile…"

Respect

He was in the Oklahoma City Airport when he saw a woman walking along with three little girls. They were skipping and singing, "Daddy's coming home on a big jet! Daddy's coming home on a big jet!" All excited! Eyes lit up like diamonds! Wild anticipation! They had never before met Daddy coming home on a jet. Their mother was so proud of them and their enthusiasm. You could see it in her eyes.

Respect

Then the plane arrived, the door opened and the passengers streamed in. You didn't have to ask which one was Daddy. The girls' bright eyes were glued on him. But his first look was for his wife and seeing her, he yelled, "Why didn't you bring my top coat?" and walked right past his adoring daughters. Here was a man who had an opportunity to be great, and he didn't recognize it.

Forty years ago, I heard Charlie Cullen tell that story and I never forgot it.

How many times a day, a week, a month, do we have the opportunity to be great through simple acts of kindness? In your Dash, never underestimate the power of a touch, a smile, a kind word, a listening ear, or an honest compliment. All have the potential to turn a life around.

*"How far you go in your life
depends on your being tender with the young,
compassionate with the aged,
sympathetic with the striving, and
tolerant of the weak and strong.
Because someday in your life you will
have been all of these."*

— George Washington Carver

"If we treat each other with respect
and more often wear a *smile*..."

Smile

Smile

Our Dash is short, but it can be wide:

A bellman made my day recently. After checking into an Atlanta hotel, Sam (his name was on his badge) picked up my two bags, gave a big smile, and said, "Isn't it a gorgeous day today?" I nodded and said, "Sure is." He then said, "I just spent the entire weekend with my two grandkids, and I can't remember when I've had more fun. Aren't kids great?" And then I added, "Sam, it seems like you're having a great day." He then looked up with a grin I'll never forget and said, "Mr. Anderson, every day above ground is a great day!"

I walked into my room feeling recharged by Sam's enthusiasm. It was obvious that he had chosen to live life to the fullest, and given the opportunity to touch someone's life in a positive way, my bet is that he took it, every time.

Every day, we all have that same opportunity to make a positive difference in the lives of others. We can choose to mope about our lot in life, or we can decide to live in awe, touching hearts along the way.

Ah, yes…we all know ducks who make lots of noise, quacking and complaining about their problems in life. And then there are eagles, who go about their business and consistently soar above the crowd.

Thanks, Sam, for soaring into my life.

"When we choose not to focus on what is missing from our lives but are grateful for the abundance that's present…we experience heaven on earth."

— SARAH BAN BREATHNACH

"So think about this long and hard;
are there things you'd like to *change*?"

Change

Over a century ago, William James, one of the founders of modern psychology, said "The great discovery of this generation is that a human being can alter their life by altering their attitude." Each day we wake up in the morning, we choose our clothes, we choose our breakfast but, most importantly, we choose our attitudes.

One of the most wonderful things about having a positive attitude is the number of people it touches, many times in ways you'll never know.

Change

In my book, *The Power of Attitude,* I told the story about going to a convenience store to get a newspaper and a pack of gum. The young woman at the check-out counter said, "That'll be five dollars please," and as I reached into my wallet, the thought occurred to me that a newspaper and gum didn't quite make it to five dollars. When I looked up to get a "re-quote," she had a big smile on her face and said, "Gotcha! I got to get my tip in there somehow!" I laughed when I knew I'd been had. She then glanced down at the paper I was buying and said, "I'm sick and tired of all this negative stuff on the front pages. I want to read some good news for a change." She then said, "In fact, I think someone should just publish a Good News newspaper – a paper with wonderful, inspiring stories about people overcoming adversity and doing good things for others. I'd buy one every day!" She then thanked me for coming in and said, "Maybe we'll get lucky tomorrow; maybe we'll get some good news," and she laughed. She made my day.

The following day, after my business appointments, I dropped by the same store again to pick up bottled water, but a different young lady was behind the counter. As I checked out I said, "Good afternoon," and handed her my money for the water. She said nothing – not a word, not a smile…nothing. She just handed me my change and in a negative tone ordered…"Next!"

It hit me right between the eyes: Two people, same age; one made me feel great, and the other, well, made me feel that I had inconvenienced her by showing up.

By the choices we make, by the attitudes we exhibit, we are influencing lives every day in positive or negative ways…our family, our peers, our friends, and even strangers we've never met before and will never meet again. So when you brush your teeth every morning, look in the mirror and ask yourself…"Are there things I'd like to change?" How will you choose to live your Dash…as "the grouch" or as "the good-news girl?" Your answer will go a long way toward determining the joy and happiness that you will experience in your life.

Change

Making a Difference

It's not the things we get but the hearts we touch that will determine our success in life. Making a difference in the lives of others is what the Dash is all about. In the end, however, the significance of our life will be determined by the choices we make. We can choose positive over negative, smiles over frowns, giving over taking and love over hate. It is only when we take responsibility for our choices that we begin to realize we truly are the masters of our fate. Only then will our lives begin to change for the better.

One of the most powerful stories about choices that I've ever read was written by Lance Wubbels in the book we wrote together, *To A Child . . . Love Is Spelled T.I.M.E.* In January of 2003, I sent the title to Lance as a possible gift book idea. Three days later, he wrote this story for the Introduction:

In the faint light of the attic, an old man, tall and stooped, bent his great frame and made his way to a stack of boxes that sat near one of the little half-windows. Brushing aside a wisp of cobwebs, he tilted the top box toward the light and began to carefully lift out one old photograph album after another. Eyes once bright but now dim searched longingly for the source that had drawn him here.

It began with the fond recollection of the love of his life, long gone, and somewhere in these albums was a photo of her he hoped to rediscover. Silent as a mouse, he patiently opened the long-buried treasures and soon was lost in a sea of memories. Although his world had not stopped spinning when his wife left it, the past was more alive in his heart than his present aloneness.

Setting aside one of the dusty albums, he pulled from the box what appeared to be a journal from his grown son's childhood. He could not recall ever having seen it before, or that his son had ever kept a journal. Why did Elizabeth always save the children's old junk? he wondered, shaking his white head.

Opening the yellowed pages, he glanced over a short entry, and his lips curved in an unconscious smile. Even his eyes brightened as he read the words that spoke clear and sweet to his soul. It was the voice of the little boy who had grown up far too fast in this very house, and whose voice had grown fainter and fainter over the years. In the utter silence of the attic, the words of a guileless six-year-old worked their magic and carried the old man back to a time almost totally forgotten.

Difference

Entry after entry stirred a sentimental hunger in his heart like the longing a gardener feels in the winter for the fragrance of spring flowers. But it was accompanied by the painful memory that his son's simple recollections of those days were far different from his own. But how different?

Reminded that he had kept a daily journal of his business activities over the years, he closed his son's journal and turned to leave, having forgotten the cherished photo that originally triggered his search. Hunched over to keep from bumping his head on the rafters, the old man stepped to the wooden stairway and made his descent, then headed down a carpeted stairway that led to the den.

Opening a glass cabinet door, he reached in and pulled out an old business journal. Turning, he sat down at his desk and placed the two journals beside each other. His was leather-

bound and engraved neatly with his name in gold, while his son's was tattered and the name "Jimmy" had been nearly scuffed from its surface. He ran a long skinny finger over the letters, as though he could restore what had been worn away with time and use.

As he opened his journal, the old man's eyes fell upon an inscription that stood out because it was so brief in comparison to other days. In his own neat handwriting were these words:

Wasted the whole day fishing with Jimmy. Didn't catch a thing.

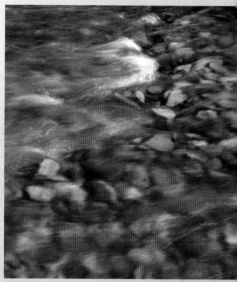

With a deep sigh and a shaking hand, he took Jimmy's journal and found the boy's entry for the same day, June 4. Large scrawling letters pressed deeply in the paper read:

Went fishing with my dad. Best day of my life.

Making

You may have heard it before but it bears repeating. Someone once said, "I've never known anyone who, on their deathbed said...I wish I had spent more time at the office."

Our Dash is a fleeting moment in time, and what we do with it is up to us. The quote on the Priorities print from Successories says it all:

"A hundred years from now it will not matter what my bank account was, the sort of house I lived in, or the kind of car I drove...but, the world may be different because I was important in the life of a child."

The Dash

BY LINDA ELLIS

While it still amazes me, a simple poem I wrote one afternoon forever changed my life. It all began when I faxed a copy of this poem to a syndicated radio show in Atlanta. Soon after receiving it, the host of this popular show read it on the air. Little did I know how much my life would change from that day forward. Titled *The Dash*, these 36 lines have touched millions of lives and have literally taken on a life of their own by traveling all over the world. I call it uncomplicated poetry in a complicated world, which became the slogan for my Internet poetry company, www.lindaellis.net.

People are always asking me what, in particular, inspired me to write this poem. I believe it was a combination of things in my life at the time. It was during a period when I was working for the top executives of a very large and successful corporation. It was a strict company with a tense working environment.

I began to watch how the priorities in many lives there had become misaligned. It seemed to me that the bosses were worrying far too much about that which was inconsequential in the scope of life.

Also, resonating in the back of my mind were the words from a letter which had been previously routed around the office. It had been written by the wife of an employee who was aware that she was dying. I was so moved by that letter that I saved a copy of it and continue to live by her words:

Regrets? I have a few. Too much worrying. I worried about finding the right husband and having children, being on time, being late and so on. It didn't matter. It all works out and it would have worked out without the worries and the tears.

The Dash

If I would have only known then what I know now. But, I did and so do you. We're all going to die. Stop worrying and start loving and living.

Her words stuck with me. Her letter made me stop and think. This is it. This is all we get.

I remember where I was when I first truly realized the significance of the piece that I had written. I was on a business trip in Minnesota, alone in a hotel room. I received an emotional email thanking me for sharing the message of the Dash from a student who had recently heard it as part of a memorial gathering for the Columbine High School students. I sat on the bed and cried.

Several years later, I found myself engulfed in the thoughts and feelings created by my own words as I listened to them read aloud, for what seemed like the very first time, at the funeral of my father…my best friend. I write this closing exactly one year from that day and never have the words of the poem meant more to me.

From being performed in an elementary school play somewhere in the heartland of America to being part of a State Supreme Court Justice's speech, from being printed in best-selling novels to high school yearbooks, *The Dash* has truly affected millions. I may not be able to change the world with these words, but I have certainly been able to influence a portion of it! The poem's words have convinced  mothers to spend more time with their children, fathers to spend more time at home, and reunited long-lost loved ones.

The words have changed attitudes, and changed the direction of lives. They have, in their own way, made a difference. I know writing *The Dash* has changed my life. I hope reading it, in some way, may change yours.

Live Your Dash,

Linda Ellis

MAC ANDERSON

MAC ANDERSON is the founder of Simple Truths and Successories, Inc., the leader in designing and marketing products for motivation and recognition. These companies, however, are not the first success stories for Mac. He was also the founder and CEO of McCord Travel, the largest travel company in the Midwest, and part owner/VP of sales and marketing for Orval Kent Food Company, the country's largest manufacturer of prepared salads.

His accomplishments in these unrelated industries provide some insight into his passion and leadership skills. He also brings the same passion to his speaking where he speaks to many corporate audiences on a variety of topics, including leadership, motivation, and team building.

Mac has authored or co-authored eighteen books that have sold over three million copies. His titles include: *Change is Good … You Go First, Charging the Human Battery, Customer Love, Finding Joy, Learning to Dance in the Rain, 212°: The Extra Degree, 212° Service, Motivational Quotes, One Choice, The Nature of Success, The Power of Attitude, The Power of Kindness, The Essence of Leadership, The Road to Happiness, The Dash, To a Child, Love is Spelled T-I-M-E, You Can't Send a Duck to Eagle School, What's the Big Idea?*

For more information about Mac, visit **www.simpletruths.com**

LINDA ELLIS

Linda Ellis started writing creatively as a child, a talent inherited from her Irish grandmother. She grew up in Florida and then moved to New York for several years. However, her southern roots kept calling her home and she settled in Georgia where she now lives with her family.

She spent many years working in the corporate environment, but after her first poem was shared on a syndicated radio program in 1994, an alternative career began to emerge and she soon came to the realization that her true passion was writing.

Because no promotion or raise received from her boss could ever equal the satisfaction she felt when she would hear from those whose hearts had been touched by her words, she made the decision to leave the corporate world behind to pursue her dream: inspiring others through her writing and speaking.

Millions of people have been touched by her words and today she shares her inspirations through her company, "Linda's Lyrics." In addition to writing, she is an inspirational speaker and makes a special connection with her audiences through her insightful and thought-provoking presentations.

Simple Truths of Life follows the success of her gift book, *The Dash, Making a Difference with Your Life,* co-authored with Mac Anderson. Her next book, *Every Single Day*, is scheduled for publication in 2011.

For more information about Linda, visit: **www.lindaellis.net**

simple truths®
THE GIFT OF INSPIRATION

If you have enjoyed this book we invite you to check out our entire collection of gift books, with free inspirational movies, at **www.simpletruths.com**.

You'll discover it's a great way to inspire *friends* and *family,* or to thank your best *customers* and *employees.*

For more information, please visit us at:
www.simpletruths.com
Or call us toll free... 800-900-3427

Making a